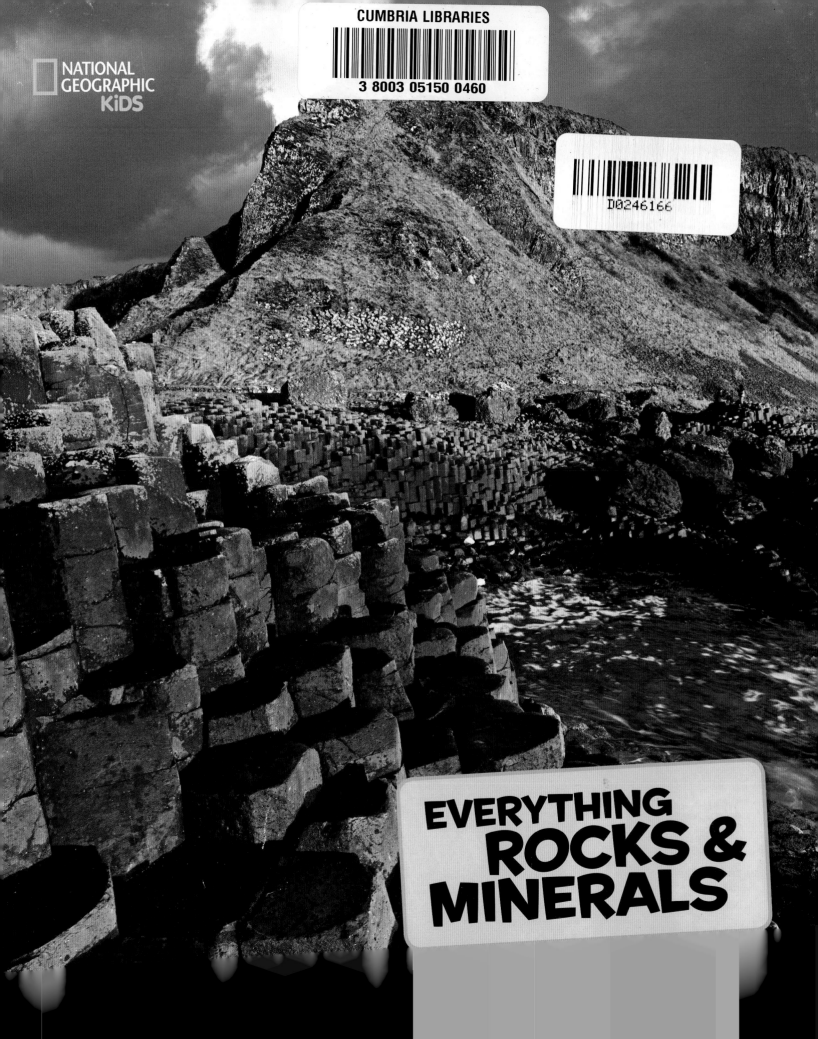

CUMBRIA LIBRARIES

3 8003 05150 0460

D0246166

NATIONAL GEOGRAPHIC KiDS

EVERYTHING ROCKS & MINERALS

NATIONAL GEOGRAPHIC KIDS

EVERYTHING
ROCKS & MINERALS

STEVE 'THE DIRTMEISTER®' TOMECEK

with National Geographic Explorer Carsten Peter

NATIONAL GEOGRAPHIC
WASHINGTON, D.C.

CONTENTS

Introduction 6

1 WORLD OF ROCKS — 8
What Is a Rock? What Is a Mineral? 10
Rock Tools, Stone Palaces 12
Digging for Treasure 14
Rocks as Resources 16
A PHOTOGRAPHIC DIAGRAM:
Rocking in our Neighbourhood 18

2 THE LIFE AND DEATH OF ROCKS — 20
Smokin' Hot Rocks 22
Masters of Change 24
Wearing Down the Rocks 26
The Rock Cycle 28
A PHOTO GALLERY: It's a Rocky World! 30

3 GEMS OF THE ROCK WORLD — 32
Crystals with Class 34
Taking a Shine to Minerals 36
Breaking Up Can Be Hard 38
Quirky Qualities 40
ROCK COMPARISONS: Before and After 42

4 FUN WITH ROCKS & MINERALS — 44
Warning: Habit Forming 46
Hunting for Treasure 48
Matching Birthstones 50
Fantastic Fossils 52
PHOTO FINISH:
Behind the Shot with Carsten Peter 54

PROTECTING OUR RESOURCES:
Afterword 56
Making Resources Last — 57
AN INTERACTIVE GLOSSARY:
Try to Rock These Words 60
Find Out More 62
Index 63
Credits 64

Circular discs of the mineral travertine surround a natural hot spring located in the Danikil Depression in Ethiopia.

Fresh natrocarbonatite lava flows over the Ol Doinyo Lengai volcano in Tanzania.

INTRODUCTION

ROCKS ARE ALL AROUND US.
MOUNTAINS ARE MADE OF ROCK AND

so are the tiny grains of sand you find on the beach. You can find them as round pebbles in streams and in the steep cliffs of valley walls. Rocks can be used for fine jewellery and turned into works of art. In the past, people used rocks as tools and weapons, and today, some of our most important natural resources come from rocks. If you were to remove all of the water and soil from the surface of the planet, all you would be left with is rock. That's because unlike Jupiter or Saturn (the gas giants), our planet is made almost entirely of rock.

While some rocks can look spectacular, with amazing colours and fantastic shapes, most simply look like, well, rocks. But a plain ordinary rock can tell an important story, if you know what to look for. When you've finished this book, you too may want to become a geologist, a scientist who studies rocks. They're the 'rock stars' of science!

EXPLORER'S CORNER

Hi! I'm Carsten Peter

and I'm what you might call an 'extreme photographer'. For the past 30 years or so, I've photographed rocks and minerals in some of the most hostile environments on Earth. As part of my work for National Geographic I've scaled the slopes of active volcanoes and explored caves deep underground. Through my pictures I try to share some of my own personal observations of the natural world. Hopefully some of my work will help inspire people like you to become a rock lover, too!

1
WORLD OF ROCKS

Thousands of years of wind and rain have sculpted the local sandstone bedrock into spectacular natural monuments at Arches National Park in Utah, U.S.A.

WHAT IS A ROCK?

This sample of quartzite is made almost entirely of the mineral quartz.

YOU MIGHT THINK OF A ROCK
AS JUST BEING COOL TO CLIMB OR THROW INTO A POND, BUT TO A GEOLOGIST THE WORD HAS A VERY

special meaning. A rock is a naturally occurring solid substance that is usually made of minerals. Some rocks are made from only a single mineral but most are made from several different minerals that have joined together. By identifying the different minerals found in a rock and by understanding the way that the minerals formed, geologists place rocks into one of three different groups. These three groups are known as igneous, metamorphic and sedimentary rocks.

These unusual features, called 'The Pinnacles', are made from weathered limestone.

NUGGET NOT ALL ROCKS FORM ON EARTH. METEORITES ARE ROCKS THAT COME FROM SPACE!

This limestone formed under water and is made mostly of the mineral calcite.

The granite (left) and the conglomerate (below) are examples of rocks that contain more than one mineral. Conglomerates, like the one found at this beach, form when pieces of other rocks are cemented together.

WHAT IS A MINERAL?

MINERALS ARE THE BUILDING BLOCKS OF

ROCKS. A MINERAL IS AN INORGANIC (NONLIVING) SOLID THAT HAS A REGULAR internal arrangement of atoms and molecules. Each mineral has its own unique combination of different chemical elements. When atoms and molecules bond together to make a mineral, they usually form some type of crystal. Every species of mineral has its own special crystal structure. Over the years scientists have discovered about 2,500 different types of minerals, but most of these are rare. In fact most of the rocks that we find are usually made from fewer than 100 common minerals.

ROCKS WITHOUT MINERALS!

Coal and amber are two types of rocks that are not made of minerals. Coal comes from plant material that has been compressed and 'cooked' over time to make a solid that burns. Amber is ancient tree sap that has hardened over time to form a solid. Both of these materials come from living things, so they are said to be organic and therefore cannot be minerals.

ROCK TOOLS, STONE PALACES

Scientists believe that the giant bluestone 'trilithons' that make up Stonehenge were built more than 4,000 years ago.

EXPLORER'S CORNER

One of the most interesting rocks that you can find near volcanoes is called obsidian. Obsidian forms when thick, gooey lava that is rich in silica flows out of a volcano and cools very quickly. I remember climbing the obsidian streams on the Italian island of Lipari and being amazed by its texture. Obsidian is an unusual rock because it has no crystals or distinctive minerals in it. Instead, it looks just like glass and is usually black, dark green or red in colour. When obsidian breaks it has razor-sharp edges. In the Stone Age, people came to Lipari to collect the obsidian and used it to make arrowheads, spear points and other cutting tools. These valuable items were then traded to other people in neighbouring regions.

EARLY IN HUMAN
HISTORY PEOPLE ONLY HAD NATURAL MATERIALS TO WORK WITH.

To help them compete with other animals, they discovered that sticks and stones could be used not only to break bones but also as tools for cutting and skinning animals. Humans began crafting choppers, scrapers and simple knives out of stone. Later they got the idea of attaching the rocks to wooden handles and created devices such as spears, sickles and axes.

When people began to settle into villages, they discovered that rocks came in handy for building sturdy structures. Unlike wood and straw that could rot or burn, rock shelters were durable and needed almost no maintenance. By moulding mud and clay into regular shapes and allowing them to dry in the sun, people made artificial rocks called bricks that could be easily stacked to form walls.

Arrowheads and other cutting tools were often made from flint and obsidian.

The Taj Mahal in India is one of the most beautiful structures on Earth. Covered in white marble and completed in 1653, it took more than 20,000 workers 22 years to build.

NUGGET THE GREAT PYRAMID IS MORE THAN 4,500 YEARS OLD AND IS MADE FROM MORE THAN 2,000,000 STONE BLOCKS.

TREASURE CHEST
Over the centuries, gems and precious metals have been collected and traded for other useful items such as food, animals and even land.

NUGGET THERE IS ENOUGH GOLD DISSOLVED IN SEAWATER TO GIVE EACH PERSON ON THE PLANET ABOUT 0.91 KILOGRAMS.

DIGGING FOR TREASURE

GEMSTONES ARE A SPECIAL
GROUP OF MINERALS WITH UNUSUAL properties that make them attractive to the eye. Some, such as diamonds, have beautiful crystal shapes. Others, such as emeralds and sapphires, have spectacular colours. Most gems have such bright colours because of the way their crystals bounce and bend light. While gems such as amethyst and garnet are fairly common, most gemstones are rare. Because of this they tend to be very valuable, and people have sought them out to use as jewellery and decorations on ceremonial items.

Precious metals such as gold, silver and platinum are also relatively rare and are valued because they are easily worked and can be turned into fine jewellery and other decorative items. Most precious metals can be found in nature, often as thin layers running through other rocks.

TURQUOISE AMULET
Frequently artisans will cut broken pieces of gemstones and use them to decorate jewellery.

GOLD BRACELET
Because it is quite soft and easy to work with, gold is one of the most important precious metals for making jewellery.

GOLD CHALICE
Not all precious metals and gems are used for jewellery. This gem-studded golden chalice was made to honour the Russian tsar, Fedor I.

ROCKS AS RESOURCES

The Kennecott Utah Copper mine, U.S.A., is one of the largest open-pit mines in the world.

NORTH AMERICA

PACIFIC OCEAN

SOUTH AMERICA

WHEN PEOPLE THINK OF NATURAL RESOURCES, ROCKS ARE NOT

usually at the top of the list, but rocks are surprisingly important resources. Most of the metals we use come from mineral ores. Iron, copper, aluminum, nickel, lead and zinc are all mined from the rocks in the ground. Much of the energy we use also comes from rocks. Fossil fuels such as coal, oil and natural gas are used to heat homes; power cars, planes and trains; and generate electricity. The truth is, you probably couldn't make it through a typical day without using a resource that originally came from a rock.

SILVER
Used for jewellery, tableware, decorative items and money. Here are the top ten silver-producing countries.

Mexico
Peru
China
Russia
Poland
Chile
Australia
Bolivia
Kazakhstan
United States

NUGGET IF YOU HEAT A DIAMOND TO 763°C, IT WILL VAPORISE.

DIAMONDS

Gem-quality diamonds are used mostly for jewellery. Here are the top ten diamond-producing countries.

Russia
Botswana
Dem. Rep. of Congo
Australia
Canada
Angola
South Africa
Zimbabwe
Namibia
Sierra Leone

ARCTIC OCEAN

EUROPE

ASIA

SALT

Used mostly for seasoning and preserving food. Here are the top ten salt-producing countries.

China
United States
India
Germany
Australia
Chile
Mexico
Canada
Brazil
Ukraine

COAL

One of the main fossil fuels, it's used to generate electricity and power factories. Here are the top ten coal-producing countries.

China
India
United States
Australia
Indonesia
Russia
South Africa
Germany
Poland
Kazakhstan

AFRICA

INDIAN OCEAN

GOLD

Used for decorative items, jewellery, and electronic components. Here are the top ten gold-producing countries.

China
Australia
Russia
United States
Canada
Peru
South Africa
Mexico
Uzbekistan
Indonesia

AUSTRALIA

IRON ORE

Used to make steel, one of the most important construction materials. Here are the top ten iron-ore-producing countries.

Australia
Brazil
China
India
Russia
Ukraine
South Africa
Canada
United States
Iran

ROCKY RESOURCES AROUND THE WORLD

Rocks are some of the most important economic resources. Each year millions of tons of minerals and coal are mined from the ground. As it turns out, these resources are not spread evenly around the globe. Here are a few of the most important mineral resources and the places they are found.

0   2,000 miles
0   2,000 kilometres

ANTARCTICA

A PHOTOGRAPHIC DIAGRAM

TV aerials can be made from copper, aluminium and iron.

Street lights can be made from a variety of metals including iron, steel and copper, all of which come from mineral ores.

MANY OF THE ITEMS
THAT WE USE EVERY DAY COME FROM
rocks and minerals. Here are a few found around an outdoor café in Edinburgh, Scotland, U.K.!

Wristwatches contain very small quartz crystals.

Many older streets are paved with cobblestones made of granite.

Curbstones are usually made from granite or marble.

Many pavements are made of flagstone, a sedimentary rock that can be split into even layers.

Traditional blackboards are made from slate, a metamorphic rock.

Older drainpipes are often made from cast iron which comes from iron ore.

Lintels over doors and windows are often made from natural stone such as sandstone or granite.

Most common types of window glass are made from quartz sand.

Jewellery is often made from precious metals such as gold and silver.

Cutlery is made from stainless steel which is made from mixing molten iron and chromium.

Drinking glasses are made by melting together silica sand with soda ash and limestone.

Outdoor furniture is often made from aluminium, which comes from the mineral ore bauxite.

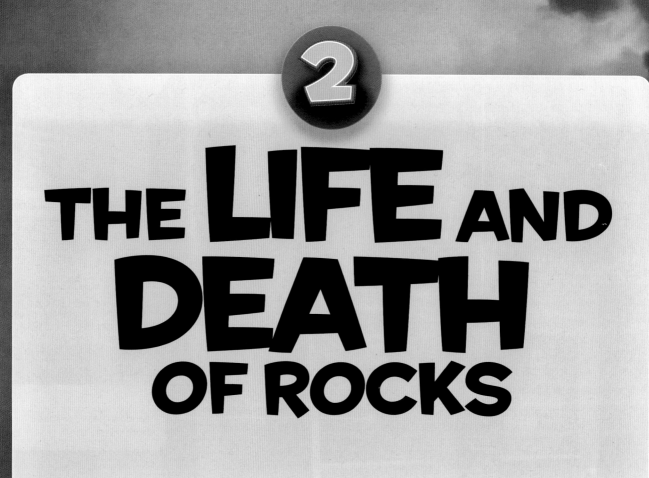

2

THE LIFE AND DEATH OF ROCKS

Red-hot lava flows out of Kilauea volcano and into the sea on the Big Island of Hawaii, U.S.A., giving birth to new rocks and creating new land in the process.

SMOKIN' HOT ROCKS

IGNEOUS ROCKS ARE THOSE THAT STARTED AS A HOT, MOLTEN LIQUID CALLED

magma. The term 'igneous' comes from a Greek word that means 'from fire'. Pools of magma form deep underground and slowly work their way to the Earth's surface. If they make it all the way, the liquid rock erupts and is called lava. As the layers of lava build up they form a mountain called a volcano. Volcanic rocks cool rather quickly so large mineral crystals don't have a chance to form. Some typical volcanic rocks include obsidian, basalt and pumice.

In many cases, magma does not have enough energy to make it all the way to the surface. Instead it begins to cool underground. This is a slow process that allows large mineral crystals to form. Rocks that form this way are called 'plutonic rocks', named after Pluto, the Roman god of the underworld. We find these rocks at the surface only after erosion has worn away the layers of rock above. Some of the most common plutonic rocks are granite, diorite and gabbro.

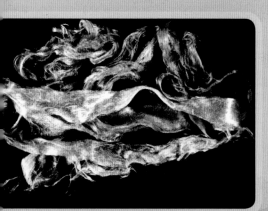

EVEN THOUGH IT LOOKS LIKE FINE THREADS, PELE'S HAIR IS ACTUALLY A VOLCANIC ROCK!

OBSIDIAN
A volcanic glass that cools so quickly that crystals can't form

ANDESITE
A fine-grained igneous rock with small crystals formed from slow-cooling lava

GRANITE PORPHYRY
A coarse-grained plutonic rock with large crystals of quartz and feldspar

GABBRO
A coarse-grained plutonic rock formed from iron and magnesium-rich magma

PUMICE
An extremely lightweight volcanic rock formed from fast-cooling lava with lots of gas

NUGGET PUMICE IS A VOLCANIC ROCK THAT IS SO CHOCK FULL OF GAS BUBBLES THAT IT ACTUALLY FLOATS IN WATER.

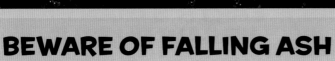

BEWARE OF FALLING ASH

Rivers of redhot lava flow down the slopes of Mount Etna in Sicily, Europe's tallest active volcano.

In addition to lava, some volcanoes also produce clouds of thick ash. Ash is made of tiny particles of rock and can cause a real problem for aeroplanes, especially if it gets in the engines. Large volcanic ash clouds can also have a chilling effect on the planet. Because the ash clouds reflect sunlight back into space, they tend to cool the surface of the Earth.

Mount Eyjafjallajökull in Iceland erupts clouds of ash in 2010.

Intensely folded
rock in a fault
zone on the
island of South
Georgia in the
Atlantic Ocean

EARTH'S GIANT JIGSAW PUZZLE

Earth's crust is not a single piece. Instead it is made up of about two dozen individual chunks called tectonic plates. These plates are in constant motion, which can produce earthquakes. When rocks get squeezed between two different plates, mountains and metamorphic rocks form.

MASTERS OF CHANGE

MICA SCHIST

Composed mostly of flaky mica minerals, which line up in parallel layers that seem to overlap each other

BANDED GNEISS

Composed of mineral grains in distinct layers or bands that often bend and fold back on themselves

MARBLE

Composed mostly of the mineral calcite, it tends to be white, but impurities will often create streaks of different colours.

SLATE

Fine-grained rock formed when the sedimentary rock shale is heated. It has many parallel layers and splits easily.

METAMORPHIC ROCKS

ARE THE MASTERS OF CHANGE! BECAUSE of intense heat and pressure deep within the Earth, these rocks have undergone a total transformation from their original form. Unlike igneous rocks, metamorphic rocks never truly melt. Instead all of the change happens in the solid state. In some cases the pressure comes from the original rocks getting buried. More often than not, the pressure comes from powerful forces caused by movements within the Earth's crust. Under these conditions, solid rock can actually flow, just like toothpaste. This results in rocks that have been twisted and bent, often with a new set of minerals in place of the old.

Most metamorphic rocks once formed the roots of ancient mountains. Because of erosion, the mountains have long since disappeared, exposing the rocks. Some typical metamorphic rocks include gneiss (pronounced 'nice'), schist and slate. Another important metamorphic rock is marble, which is used for buildings, monuments and sculptures.

THE INSIDE STORY

The Earth is not a solid planet. Instead it is made of several layers including a solid inner core, a liquid outer core, a layer of semisolid rock called the mantle, and a thin solid crust.

NUGGET THE IDEA THAT THE EARTH'S CRUST WAS MADE UP OF MOVING CONTINENTS WAS FIRST PUBLISHED BY ALFRED WEGENER IN 1912.

WEARING DOWN THE ROCKS

SEDIMENTARY ROCKS ALSO ARE THE RESULT OF CHANGE, BUT THEY FORM AT OR near the Earth's surface, which makes them very different than metamorphic rocks. Wind, water and ice constantly wear away and weather the rocks, producing smaller pieces called sediment. The terms gravel, sand, silt and clay are used to describe some of the different-sized pieces of sediment. As water flows downhill, it carries the sedimentary grains into lakes and the ocean, where they get deposited. As the loose sediment piles up, the grains eventually get compacted or cemented back together again. The result is new sedimentary rock. Sandstone, conglomerate and shale are sedimentary rocks that have formed this way.

As water runs over the surface of rocks, it also dissolves some of their minerals. A second type of sedimentary rock, called 'evaporites', forms when the water containing these dissolved minerals evaporates to form new crystals. Rock salt (halite) and gypsum are two common evaporites.

THE GRAND CANYON FORMED AFTER THOUSANDS OF YEARS OF WEATHERING AND EROSION.

SANDSTONE

As the name suggests, these rocks are made from layers of sand that have become cemented back together.

CONGLOMERATE

Looking almost like man-made concrete, these rocks are made from a random mixture of sand, silt, pebbles and clay that has hardened over time.

HALITE

Natural salt crystals that form when salt water slowly evaporates

GYPSUM

Composed of soft white gypsum crystals that form when mineral-rich water evaporates in lakes or in caves

LIMESTONE

Most often forms when the shells of creatures dissolve in sea water, forming lime mud that dries out and hardens over time

These colourful sandstones in Arizona, U.S.A., show how sedimentary rocks often form distinct layers as different types of material are deposited on top of each other.

NUGGET TO A GEOLOGIST, THE ROCK LAYERS OF THE GRAND CANYON READ LIKE THE PAGES OF A HISTORY BOOK.

THE ROCK CYCLE

SCIENTISTS ESTIMATE THAT

OUR PLANET IS ABOUT 4.6 BILLION YEARS OLD. SO FAR

the oldest rocks that have been discovered are 'only' about 4.28 billion years old. There are hardly any rocks from the early years because minerals are continuously being recycled through a process called the Rock Cycle. Here's how it works . . .

EROSION AND DEPOSITION Wind, rain and ice break down rocks to form sediment. The sediment is carried downhill and deposited in lakes and the ocean.

LITHIFICATION
Loose sediments get compacted and cemented together to form new sedimentary rocks.

EVAPORATION
Mineral-rich water evaporates, causing crystals of sedimentary rocks to grow.

NUGGET   BECAUSE OF THE ROCK CYCLE, THE OLDEST ROCKS FOUND ON EARTH ARE METEORITES FROM SPACE.

VOLCANO New igneous rocks form from cooled lava flowing out of volcanoes at the Earth's surface.

MAGMA Underground heat causes minerals to melt to form magma. Some of this magma moves to the surface to form lava, and some cools in place to form new plutonic igneous rocks.

WHILE WE CALL IT THE ROCK 'CYCLE', IN TRUTH, ROCKS CAN FORM BY ONE OF THESE PROCESSES AT ANY POINT IN THE CHAIN.

EXPLORER'S CORNER

Not all volcanoes behave the same way. Each one has its own personality, which makes them unpredictable and dangerous. Shield volcanoes, like those found in Hawaii, are formed by overlapping layers of lava. These lava flows tend to be very fluid, and unless you step in one, the danger factor is pretty low. You do have to be careful though, because the last thing you want is to get caught up in a lava flow that could be over 1,000°C!

Cinder cones are made mostly from layers of 'tephra', which are solid particles that get welded together when they land on the side of the volcano. Tephra ranges in size from tiny ash particles to chunks as big as a car. While volcanic ash may look harmless, the individual pieces can be as sharp as broken glass.

TECTONIC ACTION Rocks from the surface get buried and pushed back into the earth where they are heated and squeezed. The minerals slowly change to form metamorphic rocks.

A PHOTO GALLERY

IT'S A ROCKY WORLD!

ROCKS AND MINERALS CAN BE FOUND IN A WIDE RANGE

of different environments. In addition to being useful materials, they also give scientists clues to how our world has changed over time.

GRANITE Plutonic igneous rock rich in quartz and feldspar. It is a hard rock used as a building stone and for monuments.

BASALT Most common type of igneous rock, basalts form most of the Earth's crust under the ocean.

FOSSILS IN SHALE (ferns) Fine-grained sedimentary rock made from compacted mud. Shale often contains fossils of extinct organisms.

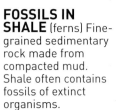

SANDSTONE Sedimentary rock that forms when sand grains get cemented back together again.

GYPSUM Sedimentary rock that forms from the evaporation of mineral-rich water.

GNEISS Coarse-grained metamorphic rock with alternating bands of different minerals created by extreme pressure.

OLIVINE This group of greenish minerals is found mainly in dark-coloured igneous rocks such as basalt, peridotite and gabbro.

BERYL Commonly found in pegmatite and schist. Well-formed green beryl crystals are also known as emeralds.

TOURMALINE Commonly found in both igneous and metamorphic rocks.

SULPHUR & SALT CRYSTALS They give the crater of Dallol volcano in Ethiopia its unique colour.

FELDSPAR Like quartz, feldspar can be found in all three major rock types.

CALCITE Found in all three rock types.

FLUORITE Most often found in igneous and metamorphic rocks.

NATIVE COPPER This soft metal forms with basalt in hydrothermal vents near volcanoes.

When they are cut and polished, diamonds sparkle and shine with remarkable colours.

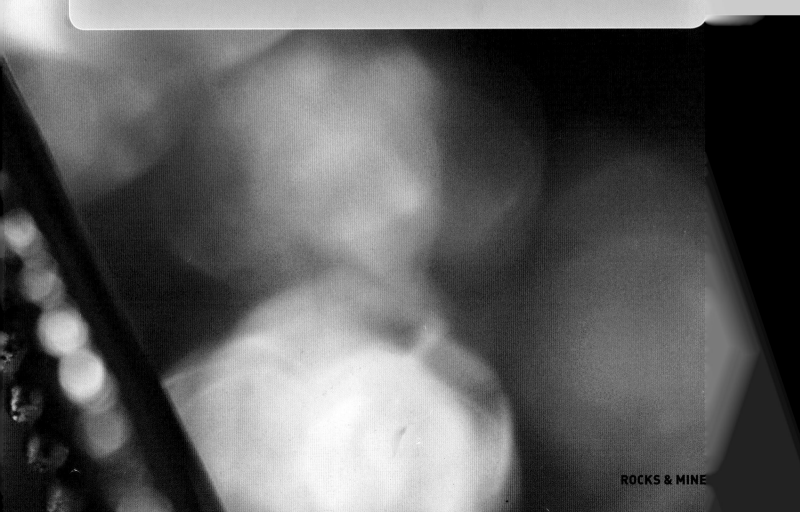

3

GEMS
OF THE
ROCK
WORLD

CRYSTALS WITH CLASS

GEOLOGISTS USE A VARIETY

OF DIFFERENT PROPERTIES TO DISTINGUISH
one mineral from another. One of the most important is
the shape of the crystal or the 'crystal habit', The shape of
a mineral's crystal is a direct result of the internal arrangement
of atoms and molecules. Each type of mineral has its own
unique crystal structure and habit. Halite, for example, will
always form crystals that look like cubes. Quartz, which has
a slightly more complex structure, forms six-sided prismatic
crystals, and garnets that have a complex formula will
generally form crystals with either 12 or 24 sides.

Well-formed crystals can only be found when conditions
are right. Often crystal growth becomes stunted, leading to
poorly formed crystals or none at all. When this happens,
geologists must use another property to help distinguish a
mineral. When the conditions are right, though, spectacular
crystals can form. Sometimes a crystal can even form 'twins',
with two perfectly formed crystals growing in opposite
directions from a single 'seed crystal'.

When you break a
geode open, it
will often have
spectacular
crystals inside.

Staurolite
crystals
often form 'twins'
growing in two different
directions at once.

When realgar (red mineral) forms crystals, they
usually appear as prisms.

The mineral
pyromorphite almost
always forms barrel-shaped
hexagonal crystals.

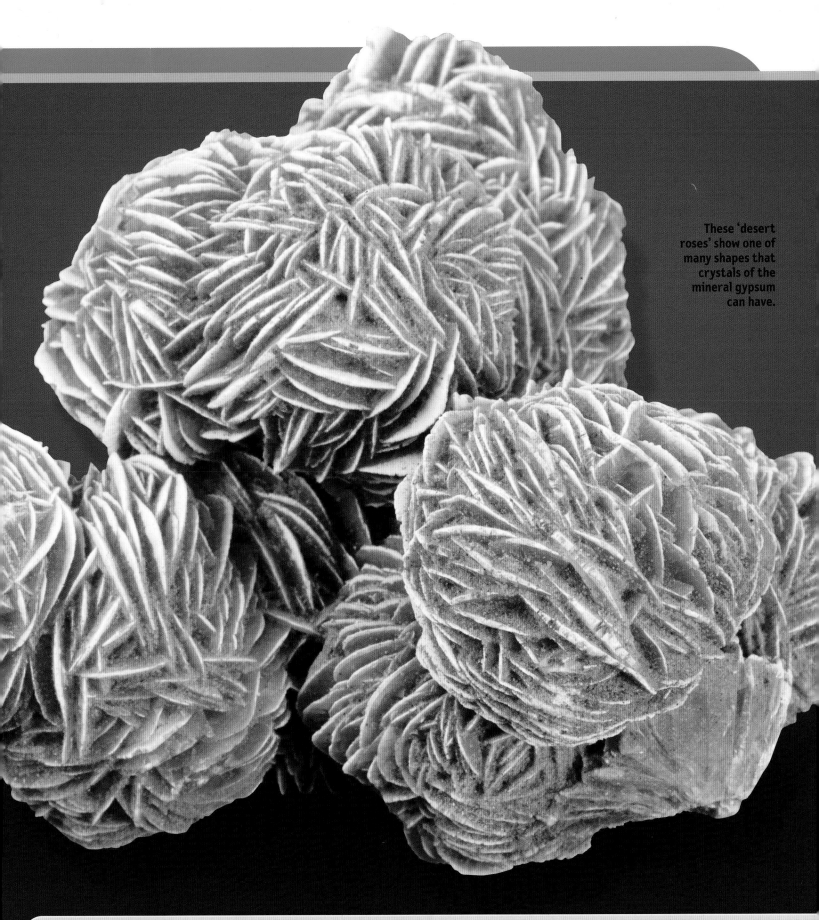

These 'desert roses' show one of many shapes that crystals of the mineral gypsum can have.

 **NUGGET** IF YOU EXAMINE THE CRYSTALS IN A SALT SHAKER WITH A MAGNIFYING GLASS, YOU WILL SEE THAT MOST LOOK LIKE LITTLE CUBES.

COLOURFUL QUARTZ

Not only is quartz the most common mineral on Earth's continents, it's also one of the most colourful! It can be white, black, grey, blue, green, yellow or red. It can also be colourless with perfectly clear, transparent crystals. Different names distinguish the different colours of quartz. Amethyst is always purple, citrine is a yellowish brown, rose quartz is pinkish-red, and smoky quartz is grey-black.

AKING A SHINE TO MINERALS

Malachite (green), azurite (blue), and ruby (red) all have very distinctive colours.

MINERALS COME IN MANY

COLOURS INCLUDING RED, YELLOW, GREEN, BLUE, purple, black, white and even clear. Some minerals are always the same colour but others, such as quartz, can come in a wide range of colours. That's why scientists also use a mineral's streak to identify it. Streak is the colour the mineral produces when it is rubbed on a special tile.

Another important property is lustre, which is how light shines off the surface of a mineral. Pyrite has a metallic lustre while quartz looks like glass. Other terms used to describe lustre include earthy, waxy, pearly and silky.

COLOUR SHOULDN'T BE THE ONLY PROPERTY USED TO IDENTIFY MINERALS. IT IS TOO VARIABLE!

The mineral pyrite or 'fool's gold' has a distinctive yellow-gold colour and shines with a metallic lustre.

NUGGET HEMATITE COMES IN MANY COLOURS BUT ALWAYS HAS A RED STREAK.

BREAKING UP CAN BE HARD

DIFFERENT MINERALS REACT IN VERY

DIFFERENT WAYS WHEN THEY ARE PUT UNDER PRESSURE.

Hardness is a measure of how resistant a mineral is to being scratched. Some minerals, such as gypsum, are so soft that you can scratch them with your fingernail. Others, such as quartz, are harder than steel. Geologists rank minerals on a scale of 1-10 using something called Mohs's Scale of Hardness.

Cleavage is the term that geologists use to describe how a mineral breaks. If you hit a chunk of salt with a hammer, it will almost always split into little cubes. Minerals in the mica family, on the other hand, can be peeled into thin sheets. The type of cleavage that a mineral has is controlled by the way the atoms in the crystal are arranged. Cleavage happens in minerals when the forces holding the atoms together in one direction are weaker than in other directions. When the forces between the atoms are equal in all directions, instead of breaking in parallel lines, the mineral fractures in a random pattern, just like a piece of glass.

The mineral muscovite mica displays a unique type of cleavage that allows the mineral to be peeled off in thin sheets.

NUGGET IN THE PAST, LARGE, THIN SHEETS OF MICA WERE ACTUALLY USED TO MAKE WINDOWS IN POTTERY OVENS.

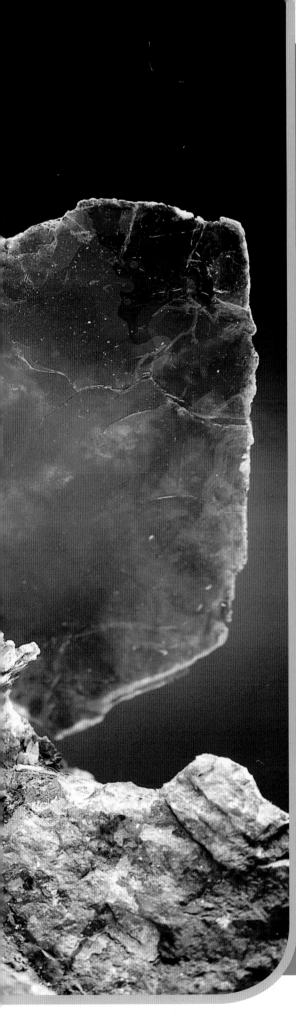

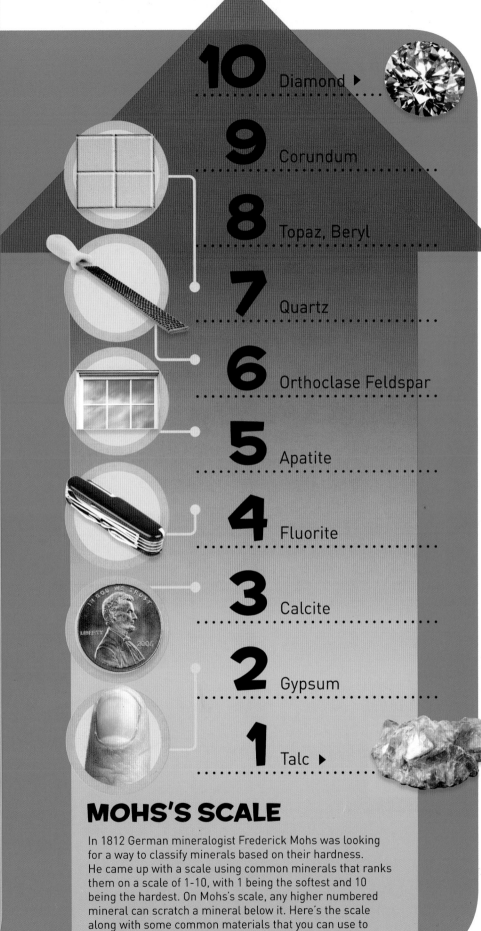

10 Diamond ▶

9 Corundum

8 Topaz, Beryl

7 Quartz

6 Orthoclase Feldspar

5 Apatite

4 Fluorite

3 Calcite

2 Gypsum

1 Talc ▶

MOHS'S SCALE

In 1812 German mineralogist Frederick Mohs was looking for a way to classify minerals based on their hardness. He came up with a scale using common minerals that ranks them on a scale of 1-10, with 1 being the softest and 10 being the hardest. On Mohs's scale, any higher numbered mineral can scratch a mineral below it. Here's the scale along with some common materials that you can use to test the hardness of minerals.

These two rocks look very different, but they are actually the same rock. The one on the left is under regular 'white' light, and the one on the right is under ultraviolet or UV light.

TOOLS OF THE TRADE

Geologists rely on a few important tools to help identify the minerals found in rocks. First they use a rock hammer to break the samples to expose fresh, un-weathered surfaces. Then they need a magnifier to get a close look at the crystals. A knife helps them get a handle on the mineral hardness, and a bottle of acid and a magnet help identify the chemical composition.

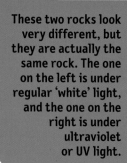

QUIRKY QUALITIES

MINERALS CAN HAVE SOME REALLY
UNIQUE PROPERTIES THAT ALLOW YOU TO IDENTIFY THEM WITH NO

trouble at all. Graphite, for example, is so soft that it feels greasy to the touch. Sulphur smells like rotten eggs, halite tastes salty, calcite will react with acid, and magnetite will stick to a magnet.

Sometimes minerals have a dull, plain colour under normal light but glow spectacularly when exposed to an ultraviolet or black light. This property is called fluorescence, and it happens in the minerals willemite and franklinite.

One of the most important mineral properties is specific gravity. This is a measure of how heavy a mineral is when it is compared to an equal amount of fresh water. Most minerals have densities that are between 2 and 5 times that of water. The mineral galena, which is an ore of lead, however, has a specific gravity of 7.5. Gold has one of the highest specific gravities. It is usually found to be more than 15 times denser than water!

EXPLORER'S CORNER

Sometimes the shape and texture of a rock can tell you a lot about how it formed. Lava flows, for instance, don't all look the same because they don't have the same properties. Pahoehoe lava (pronounced pa-'hoy-hoy) is very fluid and acts just like water in a stream, only in this case, the stream is around 1,200°C, which is hot enough to kill a person on contact. One of the scariest experiences I ever had was having to outrun a lava flow as it came pouring down the side of a volcano that I was photographing! As it cools, the flow slows down, leaving a strange surface that looks like coils of rope.

A second type of lava, called aa (pronounced 'ah-ah), is much less fluid than pahoehoe. When aa flows, it moves much more slowly and resembles hot tar or thick treacle. When the lava cools, it creates a surface with angular chunks that often have super sharp edges. If you are not careful, they can cut right through the soles of your boots!

The mineral magnetite contains a great deal of iron and is a natural magnet, so it can attract items made from steel.

NUGGET   ROCKS CONTAINING THE MINERAL CALCITE WILL FIZZ WHEN ACID IS PUT ON THEM!

ROCK COMPARISONS

BEFORE AND AFTER

BECAUSE OF THEIR VARIED

PROPERTIES, WE USE minerals for many things. When minerals are found in rocks, they look very different from their finished product. Here's a look at some common minerals and what they look like when we see them in our day-to-day lives.

Calcite is the main mineral found in limestone. Crushed limestone is used as a binder to make cement blocks.

PRECIOUS METAL

Gold is so malleable that it can be hammered into sheets that are less than 0.00002 cm thick.

FROM ROCKS TO PLUMBING

Copper ore is the natural source for the material found in pipes that keeps water flowing through buildings.

FROM ROCKS TO WALLS

Gypsum is a sedimentary mineral that is ground up and used to make plaster and plasterboard.

FROM ROCKS TO SKYSCRAPERS

Hematite is one type of iron ore that, when processed, helps hold up skyscrapers.

FROM ROCKS TO SEASONING

When ground up, halite, a natural salt, tastes great on chips.

FROM ROCKS TO CONTAINERS

Quartz sand is one of the main components of glass bottles and window panes.

FROM ROCKS TO FIRE

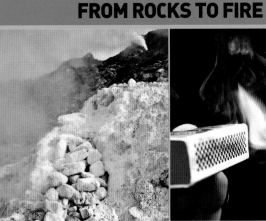

Natural sulphur is one of the important elements found in matches.

This awesome sand castle from White Beach in the Philippines shows just how fun playing with rocks can be.

4

FUN
WITH
ROCKS &
MINERALS

WARNING: HABIT FORMING

These amethyst crystals grew slowly from a liquid state.

EVERY MINERAL HAS ITS
OWN SPECIAL CRYSTAL SHAPE CALLED ITS 'HABIT'.

Mineral crystals usually begin as a liquid. As the liquid cools or evaporates, the atoms in the liquid begin to join together to form the crystal. Large well-formed crystals will only grow if the conditions are right.

SALT OF THE EARTH

In this experiment you can try your hand at growing two different types of crystals using some simple salt solutions.
Here's what you'll need:

2 small disposable clear plastic cups

Container of table salt

Container of Epsom salts (available at most chemist's)

Hot water

Permanent marker

Magnifying glass

1 Use the marker to label one cup 'plain salt' and the other 'Epsom salts'. Fill each cup about half way with hot water.

2 Stir in 5 or 6 teaspoons of table salt into the cup labelled 'plain salt' so that all the salt dissolves. Use the second spoon to do the same with the Epsom salts in the other cup.

3 Place both cups in a safe location, and allow the water to evaporate completely. It should take about a week or so.

4 After the water has completely evaporated from each cup, carefully observe the crystals that have formed on the bottom of each cup by using the magnifying glass.

You will see that the crystal habit of the table salt is little cubes, while the Epsom salt appears to be long needle-like prisms. You can experiment further by mixing different amounts of the two salts together to see what types of crystals they produce.

TABLE SALT   **EPSOM SALTS**

NUGGET WHILE THERE ARE THOUSANDS OF DIFFERENT MINERALS, THERE ARE ONLY SIX CRYSTAL SYSTEMS.

ROCKS & MINERALS **47**

HUNTING FOR TREASURE

PEOPLE ARE ALWAYS ON THE PROWL FOR NEW SOURCES OF MINERAL

resources. Everything from gemstones and precious metals to iron, copper and coal must be mined from the ground, and finding these materials is big business! Mining companies can't afford to make random guesses at where these minerals occur. Prospecting is the process of scientifically searching for valuable minerals by analysing and testing rocks. Only after geologists feel that the rocks have the potential to contain large amounts of the desired minerals can full-scale mining operations begin.

Precious metals such as gold only occur in certain rock types. Most often they are found in igneous rocks, where hot fluids concentrate them in layers called veins. Because gold has such a high specific gravity and is resistant to weathering, it is also possible to find gold nuggets that have eroded from 'host' rocks concentrated in streams and rivers. Known as placer deposits, these pockets of precious metals are the things that dreams (and fortunes) are made of! It was the discovery of a placer deposit at Sutter's Mill, California, U.S.A. that set off the great gold rush of 1849!

BECAUSE GOLD IS VERY STABLE, IT DOESN'T WEATHER AWAY LIKE OTHER MINERALS DO.

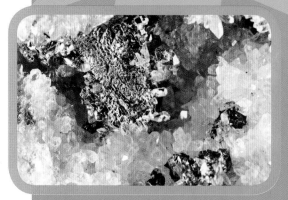

Gold can often be found as small veins running through other rocks. such as in this quartzite.

PANNING FOR GOLD

You don't need a geology degree to try your hand at being a gold prospector. All you need is a stream, some wellies, a circular metal pan and a lot of luck. Placer deposits of gold can often be found downstream of igneous rocks that have been exposed at the surface. Here's what to do:

1 Begin by finding a bend in the stream where sand and gravel have accumulated along the inner bank. Dip the pan into the water and use it to scoop up about a cup of sediment.

2 Gently swirl the pan around and allow the water to wash the lighter sediment back out of the pan. Gold is dense, so if there is any in the sediment it will sink to the bottom of the pan and begin to accumulate there.

3 After you have done this several times, use a magnifying glass to check the sediment that remains in the pan to see if you have found any gold.

Finding large gold nuggets is rare. More often than not you will only come up with tiny flakes and dust, but even these little particles tend to add up. Who knows, with a little luck you might set off a gold rush of your own!

NUGGET NOT ALL GOLD FINDS ARE SMALL. ONE GOLD NUGGET FOUND IN CALIFORNIA WEIGHED A WHOPPING 73 KILOGRAMS.

MATCHING BIRTHSTONES

IN THE PAST, PEOPLE BELIEVED THAT CERTAIN GEMS BROUGHT good luck to those people born in different months and that these gems stood for special qualities in a person. The chart below lists the primary birthstone for each month as well as the unique character trait that it represents in a person.

	Month		Stone	Character Trait
1	January		Garnet	Constancy
2	February		Amethyst	Sincerity
3	March		Aquamarine	Courage
4	April		Diamond	Innocence
5	May		Emerald	Love and Success
6	June		Moonstone	Health and Longevity
7	July		Ruby	Contentment
8	August		Peridot	Married Happiness
9	September		Sapphire	Clear Thinking
10	October		Pink Tourmaline	Hope
11	November		Citrine	Fidelity
12	December		Blue Topaz	Prosperity

MATCH GAME

How's your eye at spotting a gemstone? Can you tell what your birthstone looks like before it is cut and polished? In the column to the left are the twelve birthstones the way they would look in a jewellery store. Below are the same 12 gems as they appear in nature. See if you can match the finished stone with its natural counterpart.

A

B

G

H

ANSWERS: 1E, 2K, 3C, 4I, 5A, 6G, 7F, 8L, 9D, 10J, 11B, 12H

CUTTING AND POLISHING

Gemstones in the field hardly ever look like a gem. Instead they usually look dull, with rough edges, and often resemble plain, ordinary rocks. Before a gemstone can be considered a gem, it usually has to be worked. A lapidary is the person who cuts, polishes and engraves stones in order to make them look more attractive.

A lapidary uses a polishing wheel to finish a gemstone.

NUGGET   PEOPLE ONCE BELIEVED THAT WEARING EMERALDS COULD PREVENT EPILEPSY, STOP BLEEDING AND EVEN CURE DIARRHOEA!

FANTASTIC FOSSILS

FOOD FIND

Coprolites or fossil animal dung can give paleontologists an idea of the type of food that an extinct animal ate.

ONE OF THE MOST EXCITING

THINGS TO FIND IN A ROCK IS A FOSSIL. A FOSSIL IS any evidence of a once-living thing that is preserved in stone. It comes in many forms. A fossil can be the print of a leaf, a cast of a shell, a piece of petrified wood, or an insect preserved in amber. Some of the coolest fossils are dinosaur bones. These are often preserved when mineral-rich water fills in the tiny pores found in the bone after they have become buried in the ground. Fossils are usually found in sedimentary rock such as limestone, shale and sandstone. Because of the way that fossils form, the most common types are the hard parts of animals and plants, such as bones, teeth and seeds. Not all fossils contain the actual parts of the plants or animals. Footprints, burrows and tracks are all considered to be 'trace fossils'. So are coprolites, which are fossilised pieces of animal dung that have turned to stone!

FRIENDS FOREVER

These trilobite fossils give scientists a clue of what sea creatures looked like on Earth more than half a billion years ago.

Seashell that has a textured surface	Chunk of plastic modeling clay	Oil-based cooking spray	Pre-mixed plaster or spackling compound	Plastic teaspoon	Roll of paper towels

 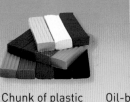  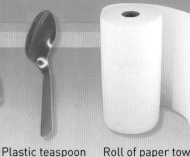

MAKE YOUR OWN FOSSIL

Some of the most common fossils that people find are moulds and casts. The way they form is that a hard body part, such as a shell or bone, gets buried in the mud and the mud turns to stone. The original material then dissolves away leaving an exact imprint in the stone. This is called the mould. The mould then gets filled in with new material, which then hardens to form an exact copy of the original animal part. This is called the cast. Try making your own mould and cast using some simple materials.

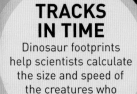

TRACKS IN TIME
Dinosaur footprints help scientists calculate the size and speed of the creatures who left them.

1 Work the clay in your hands so that it becomes soft, and then roll it into a ball. Squeeze it into a fat pancake and place it on a paper towel.

2 Place the shell on a second paper towel, and coat the outer surface lightly with cooking spray. Take the shell and turn it upside down. Gently press the outer surface into the clay and remove it. You should be left with an exact imprint of the shell (the mould).

3 Use the teaspoon to fill the mould with wet plaster, making sure to pack it down so it fills all the spaces. Place the clay with the plaster in a safe place and allow it to dry for 2 days.

4 After the plaster has dried, remove the clay and look at the cast of the shell. Compare it to the original shell to see how much detail your fossil copy has.

NUGGET   SOME COPROLITES ARE SO WELL PRESERVED THAT SCIENTISTS CAN TELL WHAT THE ANIMAL HAD EATEN!

PHOTO FINISH

WHEN YOU ARE
EXPLORING CAVES, THERE'S NO

telling what you might find. Here's one of the shots that I took inside a Mexican cave called Cueva de los Cristales or Cave of Crystals. Those little red things that look like bugs crawling around are some of the scientists that I was travelling with, and what they are climbing on are gigantic gypsum crystals.

The Cave of Crystals was discovered accidentally by two brothers in 2000. They were looking for silver and zinc, which are common in the area, but what they found instead were some of the largest crystals ever discovered. Some of the larger ones weigh as much as 50 tons and stretch over 11.4 metres long.

Cueva de los Cristales was very cool to explore, but it's anything but cool inside. A pool of magma located about a kilometre and a half beneath the cave keeps it a toasty 45ºC inside. It was a combination of this high temperature and stable environment that allowed the crystals to grow to be so large.

To work in such a hostile environment meant that I had to take special precautions. To keep from overheating, I wore a special vest filled with ice packs. In order to keep breathing, I had to wear a special respirator that chilled the air going to my lungs. To top it all off, I had to wear a jumpsuit, helmet, special boots and gloves. All this equipment made it really difficult to take pictures but without it, I wouldn't have been able to last more than a dozen minutes before I passed out or suffered heat stroke.

Gigantic crystals of selenite gypsum dwarf explorers in the Cave of Crystals in Mexico.

AFTERWORD

PROTECTING OUR RESOURCES

ROCKS AND MINERALS
ARE INCREDIBLY IMPORTANT RESOURCES

that we humans just can't live without. Unfortunately the act of mining rocks and minerals can also create some serious problems. When mines are dug underneath the ground, the rocks above them often become unstable, which can cause a mine to collapse. In addition, if the mine isn't properly ventilated, dust and gases that build up in the mine can cause it to explode. This can lead to loss of life for both the miners and the people living in the surrounding area. Even when conditions are good, miners face many health and safety problems due to long-term exposure to dust and toxic chemicals.

If the desired mineral resources are close enough to the surface, many mining companies use strip mines instead of tunnelling below the ground. As the name suggests, a strip mine is a mine where all the surface rock is removed. While strip mines are much safer than subsurface mines, they have a devastating impact on the local environment. Sometimes entire mountains are removed and replaced by large piles of mining debris. Water running through these mines can pollute streams, rivers and groundwater resources. When the debris piles get saturated with rainwater, they can cause mudflows and floods.

One way of cutting down on the amount of new minerals that have to be mined is to recycle used materials. These cars will eventually be turned back into new products.

MAKING RESOURCES LAST

ONE OF THE BIGGEST PROBLEMS we face with mineral resources is that they are almost all considered to be nonrenewable resources. This means that either they are not currently being created by natural processes anymore, or they form too slowly to replace the resources that we use. Some of these resources are beginning to run out. Rather than continue with business as usual, we need to change some of our old habits. Instead of disposing of products in landfills when they are worn out, we have to actively recycle the mineral resources that they contain. If we all pitch in and do our part, we will be able to make the most out of the mineral resources that we have so that future generations will be able to continue to share them too!

Strip mines use gigantic machines to literally move entire mountains. Here a bucket-wheel excavator in Germany removes material from the surface to reach the coal below.

Located in central Australia, Uluru/Ayers Rock is a giant sandstone monolith that has really stood the test of time. It is sacred to the local aboriginal people.

AN INTERACTIVE GLOSSARY

THESE WORDS ARE

COMMONLY USED BY geologists. Use the glossary to see what each word means, and visit its page numbers to see the word used in context. Then test your knowledge to see if you really are a 'rock star'.

Cleavage
(PAGE 38)
How a mineral breaks.

If you hit mica with a hammer it will break into _____.
a. Thin sheets
b. Cubes
c. Random pieces
d. Spheres

Conglomerate
(PAGE 26)
Sedimentary rock made from a random mixture of sand, silt, pebbles and clay.

Conglomerate looks similar to man-made _____.
a. Concrete
b. Plastic
c. Steel
d. Sand

Crystal Habit
(PAGE 34)
The shape of a crystal.

The crystal habit helps geologists _____.
a. Name a mineral
b. Distinguish between two different minerals
c. Find a mineral
d. All of the above

Deposition
(PAGE 28)
When sediment is deposited in lakes or oceans.

Sediment enters lakes and oceans _____.
a. Dissolved in water
b. After erosion
c. At river deltas
d. All of the above

An explorer crawls through one of the many Madre de Dios island caves in Chile.

Fluorescence
(PAGES 40-41)
The property of a dull, plain-coloured mineral to glow under ultraviolet light.

Fluorescence is _____.
a. A common property of minerals
b. Not helpful in identifying minerals
c. One of the most helpful properties when identifying a mineral
d. None of the above

Hardness
(PAGES 38-39)
The measure of how resistant a mineral is to being scratched.

According to Mohs's Scale of Hardness, what is the hardest mineral?
a. Diamond
b. Talc
c. Quartz
d. None of the above

Igneous Rock
(PAGES 22-23)
Rocks formed by the cooling and solidification of hot magma as it moves toward the Earth's surface.

Which igneous rock was often used for arrowheads and sharp tools during the Stone Age?
a. Andesitic
b. Obsidian
c. Pumice
d. Gabbro

Inorganic
(PAGE 11)
nonliving. An inorganic rock is made up of one or multiple minerals, whereas an organic rock is made up of materials that were once living but have been compressed and 'cooked' over time.

Which of the following rocks is inorganic?
a. Coal
b. Amber
c. Graphite
d. None of the above

Lithification
(PAGE 28)
The compaction and cementation of loose sediment into new sedimentary rocks.

Between which two events in the Rock Cycle does lithification occur?
a. After erosion and before deposition
b. After deposition and before erosion
c. After erosion and before evaporation
d. After evaporation and before erosion

Lustre
(PAGES 36-27)
How light shines off the surface of a mineral.

Which of the following does not have a glassy lustre?
a. Gold
b. Diamond
c. Ruby
d. Quartz

Magma
(PAGES 22-23)
Hot molten liquid rock below the Earth's surface.

What is magma called if it erupts at the Earth's surface?
a. Plutonic Magma
b. Pumice
c. Ash
d. Lava

Metamorphic Rock
(PAGES 24-25)
Rock that while in its solid form has undergone a complete transformation due to intense pressure and heat deep within the Earth.

Which famous structure is made almost entirely of metamorphic rock?
a. The Pyramids in Egypt
b. Edinburgh Castle, Scotland, U.K.
c. The Great Wall of China
d. The Parthenon in Greece

Plutonic Rock
(PAGE 22)
Rock made up of large mineral crystals that form as magma cools and solidifies slowly below the Earth's surface.

This type of rock was named after Pluto, the Greek god of:
a. The Underworld
b. Fire
c. Rock
d. The Earth

Sediment
(PAGE 26)
Small pieces of rock that break off larger rocks that have been weathered and worn away by wind, water or ice.

Which of the following are examples of sediment?
a. Sand beaches
b. Gravel driveways
c. Clay pots
d. All of the above

Sedimentary Rocks
(PAGES 26-27)
Rock formed at the Earth's surface from sediment that has piled up and cemented back together or from the evaporation of water containing sediment.

Sedimentary rock is often _____.
a. Sharp and jagged
b. Warm to the touch
c. Layered
d. All of the above

Specific Gravity
(PAGE 41)
The measure of how heavy a mineral is when it is compared to equal volume of fresh water.

Most minerals have a specific gravity between _____.
a. -3 and 0
b. 2 and 5
c. 8 and 10
d. 10 and 15

ANSWERS: Cleavage: a; Conglomerate: a; Crystal Habit: b; Deposition: d; Hardness: c; Fluorescence: c; Igneous Rock: b; Inorganic: c; Lithification: b; Lustre: a; Magma: d; Metamorphic Rock: d; Plutonic Rock: a; Sediment: d; Sedimentary Rocks: c; Specific Gravity: b

FIND OUT MORE

If you want to dig a little deeper to get the inside dirt on rocks and minerals, check out some of these other books and websites.

BOOKS THAT SPARKLE

Rocks and Minerals: A Gem of a Read
BY DAN GREEN AND SIMON BASHER
Kingfisher, 2009

The Rock Factory: The Story About the Rock Cycle
BY JACQUI BAILEY
Picture Window Books, 2006

National Geographic Visual Encyclopedia of Earth
BY MICHAEL ALLABY
National Geographic, 2008

Jump Into Science: Rocks & Minerals
BY STEVE TOMECEK
National Geographic, 2010

Eye Wonder: Rocks and Minerals
BY CAROLINE BINGHAM
Dorling Kindersley, 2004

Eyewitness: Rock and Mineral
BY R.F. SYMES
Dorling Kindersley, 2008

WEBSITES THAT ROCK!

Mineralogy 4 Kids
Mineralogical Society of America
www.minsocam.org/MSA/K12/K_12.html

Rockwatch
The UK's national geology club for children
https://www.rockwatch.org.uk/

Geoscience Australia
Classroom resources
http://www.ga.gov.au/education/classroom-resources

Webmineral
A comprehensive mineral database
http://webmineral.com/

National museum of natural history
Over 5000 rocks and minerals
http://www.nhm.ac.uk/our-science/collections/mineralogy-collections.html

Geology Rocks
Fun kids live with the geological society
http://www.funkidslive.com/learn/geology-rocks/

Photo Credits
COVER, Mark Thiessen/ NationalGeographicStock.com; BACK COVER, Sebastian Janicki/ Shutterstock.com; 1, Chris Hill/ NationalGeographicStock.com; 2-3, David Evans/ NationalGeographicStock.com; 5, Carsten Peter/ NationalGeographicStock.com; 6, Carsten Peter/ NationalGeographicStock.com; 7 (top), Jason Tharp; 7 (bottom), Carsten Peter/ NationalGeographicStock.com; 8-9, Bruce Dale/ NationalGeographicStock.com; 10 (top, left), Susan E. Degginger/ Alamy; 10 (bottom, left), Image Source/ Corbis; 10, (background), paterne/ iStockphoto; 10 (bottom, right), Wally Eberhart/ Visuals Unlimited/ Getty Images; 11, (top, left), Eye Ubiquitous/ Rex USA; 11 (top, center), Paul Seheult/ Eye Ubiquitous/ Alamy; 11 (top, right), Marli Miller/ Visuals Unlimited/ Corbis; 11 (center), Jason Tharp; 11 (background), Duncan Walter/ iStockphoto; 11 (bottom, above), kkymek/ Shutterstock; 11 (bottom), Jeff Daly/ Visuals Unlimited/ Getty Images; 12 (top), Bryan Busovicki/ Shutterstock; 12 (left), Jason Tharp; 12 (right), Kenneth V. Pilon/ Shutterstock; 13, Lori Epstein/ NationalGeographicStock.com; 13 (bottom, right), sculpies/ Shutterstock; 14, Zoran Vukmanov Simokov/ Shutterstock; 14 (inset), Susan S. Carroll/ Shutterstock; 15, (bottom, left), Sandro Vannini/ Corbis; 15 (bottom, centre), Myotis/ Shutterstock; 15 (centre), O. Louis Mazzatenta/ NationalGeographicStock.com; 15 (top, right), Cary Wolinsky/ NationalGeographicStock.com; 15 (far right), Andrey Savelyev/ 123RF.com; 16 (left), James P. Blair/ NationalGeographicStock.com; 16 (right), Margaret M. Stewart/ Shutterstock; 17 (top, left), leolintang/ Shutterstock; 17 (bottom, left), Gina Sanders/ Shutterstock; 17 (top, right), Smit/ Shutterstock; 17 (centre, right), David W. Hughes/ Shutterstock; 17 (bottom, right), Denis Selivanov/ Shutterstock; 18-19, Iain Sharp/Alamy ; 20-21, Pete Orelup/ Flickr/ Getty Images; 22 (top, left), Bettmann/ Corbis; 22 (bottom, left), Visuals Unlimited/ Getty Images; 22 (right, all), Visuals Unlimited/ Getty Images; 23 (top), Carsten Peter/ NationalGeographicStock.com; 23 (bottom, right), J. Helgason/ Shutterstock; 24 (top), Ralph Lee Hopkins/ NationalGeographicStock.com; 24 (bottom), Gary Hincks/ Photo Researchers, Inc.; 25 (left) top to bottom: Visuals Unlimited/ Corbis; Dirk Wiersma/ Photo Researchers, Inc.; Doug Martin/ Photo Researchers, Inc.; DEA/ C.Dani/ Getty Images; 25 (right), Roger Harris/ Photo Researchers, Inc.; 26 (left), Chee-Onn Leong/ Shutterstock; 26 (right) top to bottom: Michal Baranski/ Shutterstock; Wally Everhart/ Visuals Unlimited/ Corbis; Theodore Clutter/ Photo Researchers, Inc.; Terry Davis/ Shutterstock; Charles D. Winters/ Photo Researchers, Inc.; 27, Leene/ Shutterstock; 28, Gary Hincks/ Photo Researchers, Inc.; 29 (top and bottom), Gary Hincks/ Photo Researchers, Inc.; 29 (right), Jason Tharp; 30 (top, left), Panoramic Stock Images/ NationalGeographicStock.com; 30 (top, right), Jim Richardson/ NationalGeographicStock.com; 30 (centre, left), Ted Clutter/ Photo Researchers, Inc.; 30 (bottom, left), Jim Lopes/ Shutterstock; 30 (bottom, centre), Charles D. Winters/ Photo Researchers, Inc.; 30 (bottom, right), Andreas Strauss/ Look/ Getty Images; 31 (top, left), Scenics & Science/ Alamy; 31 (top, right), Mark A. Schneider/ Photo Researchers, Inc.; 31 (centre, left), Visuals Unlimited/ Corbis; 31 (centre, right), Carsten Peter/ NationalGeographicStock.com; 31 (bottom, left), Goran Bogicevic/ Shutterstock; 31 (bottom, centre, above), Dirk Wiersma/ Photo Researchers, Inc.; 31 (bottom, centre, below), Arturo Limon/ Shutterstock; 31 (bottom, right), PHOTO 24/ Getty Images; 32-33, Steve Taylor/ Stone/ Getty Images; 34 (left), Gary Cook, Inc./ Visuals Unlimited/ Corbis; 34 (top, right), CLM/ Shutterstock; 34 (centre, right), Scenics & Science/ Alamy; 34 (bottom, right), Visuals Unlimited/ Corbis; 35, Visuals Unlimited/ Corbis; 36 clockwise from top left: Nikolai Pozdeev/ Shutterstock; Martin Novak/ Shutterstock; Bakalusha/ Shutterstock; Yashuhide Fumoto/ Photodisc/ Getty Images; Madeleine Openshaw/ Shutterstock; DEA/ G.Cigolini/ Getty Images; Vinicius Tupinamba/ Shutterstock; 37 (left), Charles D. Winters/ Photo Researchers, Inc.; 37 (top, right), Buquet Christophe/ Shutterstock; 37 (centre, right), Pablo Romero/ Shutterstock; 37 (bottom, right), Corbin17/ Alamy; 37, Charles D. Winters/ Photo Researchers, Inc.; 38 (left) top to bottom: Naturaldigital/ Shutterstock; Serg64/ Shutterstock; Travis Manley/ Shutterstock; Ivan Montero Martinez/ Shutterstock; Vladimir Wrangel/ Shutterstock; Aaron Amat/ Shutterstock; 39 (top, right), South12th Photography/ Shutterstock; 39 (bottom, right), Manamana/ Shutterstock; 40 (top, both), Mark A. Schneider/ Photo Researchers, Inc.; 40 (bottom) left to right: funkypoodle/ Shutterstock; HomeStudio/ Shutterstock; Carol & Mike Werner/ Index Stock Imagery/ Photolibrary; Shootz Photography/ Shutterstock; Maria Jeffs/ iStockphoto; 41 (left), Visuals Unlimited/ Getty Images; 41 (right), Jason Tharp; 42 (top), Vitaly Raduntsev/ Shutterstock; 42 (bottom), Katia/ Shutterstock; 43 (top, far left), Ken Lucas/ Visuals Unlimited/ Corbis; 43 (top, centre left), David Burrows/ Shutterstock; 43 (top, centre right), Buhantsov Alexey/ Shutterstock; 43 (top, far right), Jill Battaglia/ Shutterstock; 43 (centre, far left), DEA/ A.Rizzi/ Getty Images; 43 (centre, centre left), Joe Gough/ Shutterstock; 43 (centre, centre right), Borislav Dopudja/ Alamy; 43 (centre, far right), cardiae/ Shutterstock; 43 (bottom, far left), Eastimages/ Shutterstock; 43 (bottom, centre left), Eduard Steimakh/ Shutterstock; 43 (bottom, centre right), Luisa Puccini/ Shutterstock; 43 (bottom, far right), Mudassar Ahmed Dar/ Shutterstock; 44-45, Bildagentur RM/ Tips Italia/ Photolibrary; 46, Mark Schneider/ Visuals Unlimited/ Corbis; 47 (top) left to right: Dzarek/ Shutterstock; John Madden/ iStockphoto; Leonard Lessin/ Peter Arnold Images/ Photolibrary; Danny Smythe/ Shutterstock; Trinacria Photo/ Shutterstock; Smit/ Shutterstock; 47 (bottom, left), Kevin Schafer/ Peter Arnold Images/ Alamy; 47 (bottom, right), Dai Haruki/ Flickr/ Getty Images; 48 (left), Dirk Wiersma/ Photo Researchers, Inc.; 48 (right), George Allen Penton/ Shutterstock; 49 Antonio V. Oquias/ Shutterstock; 50 (left, all), JewelryStock/ Alamy; 50 (A), Manamana/ Shutterstock; 50 (B), Jens Mayer/ Shutterstock; 50 (G), PjrStudio/ Alamy; 50 (H), E.R. Degginger/ Photo Researchers, Inc.; 51 (top), Palani Mohan/ Getty Images; 51 (top, inset), Amritaphotos/ Alamy; 51 (C), Alexander Maksimov/ Shutterstock; 51 (D), Biophoto Assoc./ Photo Researchers, Inc.; 51 (E), DEA/ C. Bevilacqua/ Getty Images; 51 (F), DEA/ A.Rizzi/ Getty Images; 51 (I), DEA/ C. Bevilacqua/ Getty Images; 51 (J), DEA/ Getty Images; 51 (K), Suponev Vladimir/ Shutterstock; 51 (L), Mark A. Schneider/ Photo Researchers, Inc.; 52 (top, left), Scientifica/ Visuals Unlimited/ Getty Images; 52 (centre, left), Albert Lleal/ Minden Pictures/ NationalGeographicStock.com; 52 (bottom) left to right: Dr. Margorius/ Shutterstock; ra3rn/ Shutterstock; Daniel Dillon/ Alamy; Mark Herreid/ Shutterstock; Mudassar Ahmed Dar/ Shutterstock; Steve Collender/ Shutterstock; 53 (top), Matthias Breiter/ Minden Pictures/ NationalGeographicStock.com; 53 (bottom), Fotosearch/ SuperStock; 55, Carsten Peter/ Speleoresearch & Films/ NationalGeographicStock.com; 56 (bottom), Pete Ryan/ NationalGeographicStock.com; 57, Régis Bossu/ Sygma/ Corbis; 58-59, Art Wolfe/ artwolfe.com; 60, Carsten Peter/ NationalGeographicStock.com.

BOLDFACE INDICATES ILLUSTRATIONS.

A

Aa lava 41
Aluminium 18
Amber 11, **11**
Amethyst 15, 36, 46, **46–47**, 50, **50**
Andesite 22, **22**
Aquamarine 50, **50**
Arches National Park, Utah, U.S.A. **8–9**, 9
Arrowheads 12, **12**
Ayers Rock, Australia 58, **58–59**
Azurite 37, **37**

B

Basalt 22, 30, **30**, 31
Beryl 31, **31**, 39
Birthstones 50–51, **50–51**
Blackboards 18, **19**
Blue topaz 50, **50**
Bluestone 12, **12**
Bricks 12

C

Calcite (mineral) 10, 25, 31, **31**, 39, 41, 42
Cars, recycling 56, **56**
Caves 54, **54–55**, **60–61**, 61
Citrine 36, 50, **50**
Clay 26
Cleavage 38
Coal 11, **11**, 17, **17**
Conglomerates 11, **11**, 26, **26**
Continents, movement 25
Copper 18, 31, **31**, 43, **43**
Coprolites 52, **52**, 53
Crystal habit 34, 47
Crystal systems 47
Crystals 11, 15, 34, **34**, 38, 47, 54, **54–55**
Cueva de los Cristales, Mexico 54, **54–55**

D

Dallol (volcano), Ethiopia 31, **31**
Danikil Depression, Ethiopia **4–5**, 5
Deposition 28
Diamonds 15, 17, **17**, 32, **32–33**, 39, 50, **50**
Dinosaur footprints 53, **53**
Dung, fossilised 52, **52**, 53

E

Earth
    age 28
    crust 24, **24**, 25
    layers 25, **25**
Edinburgh, Scotland, U.K. **18–19**
Emeralds 15, 31, 50, **50**, 51
Epsom salt 47, **47**
Erosion 25, 28
Etna, Mt. (volcano), Sicily, Italy **22–23**, 23
Evaporation 28
Evaporites 26
Eyjafjallajökull, Mt. (volcano), Iceland 23, **23**

F

Fault zones 24, **24–25**
Feldspar 22, 31, **31**
Fluorescence 41
Fluorite 31, **31**, 39
Footprints, fossil 52, 53, **53**
Fossils 30, **30**, **52**, 52–53

G

Gabbro 22, **22**, 31
Garnets 15, 34, 50, **50**
Gems 14, **14**, 15, **15**, 50–51, **50–51**, 51
Geodes 34, **34**
Glass 19, **19**, 43, **43**
Gneiss 25, **25**, 30, **30**
Gold **17**
    malleability 42
    mining & prospecting 17, 48, 49
    panning for 48, **48**, **48–49**
    in seawater 14
    specific gravity 41
    uses 15, **15**, 17
Grand Canyon, Arizona, U.S.A. 26, **26**, 27
Granite 11, **11**, 19, 22
Granite porphyry 22, **22**
Great Pyramid, Egypt 13, **13**
Gypsum **26**, **30**
    in building materials 43, **43**
    crystals **34–35**, 35
    formation 26, 30
    hardness 38, 39
    selenite 54, **54–55**

H

Halite 26, **26**, 34, 41, 43, **43**
Hardness scale 38, 39
Hematite 37, 43, **43**

I

Igneous rocks 10, 22, 29
Iron 17, **17**, 19, 22, 41

K

Kilauea (volcano), Hawaii, U.S.A. **20–21**, 21

L

Lapidary 51, **51**
Lava **6–7**, 12, **20–21**, 21, 22, **22**, **22–23**, 23, 29, **29**, 41
Limestone 10, **10**, 19, 26, **26**, 42, **42–43**
Lithification 28

M

Madre de Dios Island caves, Chile **60–61**, 61
Magma 22, 29, **29**
Magnetite 41, **41**
Malachite 37, **37**
Map 16–17
Marble 13, **13**, 18, 25, **25**
Matches 43, **43**
Metals 14, 15, 16, **18**, 18–19, **18–19**
Metamorphic rocks 10, 24, 25, **25**, 29
Meteorites 10, 28
Mica 25, **25**, 38, **38–39**
Minerals
    cleavage 38
    colours **36–37**, 37
    crystal habit 34, 47
    definition 11
    evaporites 26
    every day use 18–19, **18–19**, 42–43, **42–43**
    hardness 38
    identification 34, 37, 41
    under light 40, **40**, **40–41**, 41
    properties 41
    as resources 16–17, **16–17**
Mines and mining 16, **16**, 48, 56, **56–57**, 57
Mohs, Frederick 39
Mohs's Scale of Hardness 38, 39
Moonstone 50, **50**
Mountains 24, 25
Muscovite mica 38, **38–39**

N

Natrocarbonatite lava **6–7**
Natural resources
    map 16–17
    protection 56–57

O

Obsidian 12, 22, **22**
Ol Doinyo Lengai (volcano), Tanzania 6, **6–7**
Olivine 31, **31**

P

Pahoehoe lava 41
Pavements 18, **18**
Pele's hair 22, **22**
Peridot 50, **50**
Peter, Carsten 7, **7**
Pink tourmaline 50, **50**
Plate tectonics 24, **24**, 29, **29**
Plumbing materials 43, **43**
Plutonic rocks 22, 29, 30
Prisms 34, **34**
Prospecting 48
Pumice 22, **22**
Pyramids 13, **13**
Pyrite 37, **37**
Pyromorphite 34, **34**

Q

Quartz
    colours 36, **36–37**
    crystal habit 34
    in glass 18, 19, 43, **43**
    in granite porphyry 22
    hardness 38, 39
    lustre 37
    in quartzite 10
Quartzite 10, **10**

R

Realgar 34, **34**
Recycling 56, **56**, 57
Resources, natural
    map 16–17
    protection 56–57
Rock cycle 28–29, **28–29**
Rock salt 26, **26**, 34, 41, 43, **43**
Rocks
    definition 10
    every day use 18–19, **18–19**
    groups 10
Rose quartz 36
Rubies 37, **37**, 50, **50**

S

Salt 17, **17**, 31, 35, 38, 47, **47**
    see also Halite
Sand 19, 26, 44, **44–45**
Sandstone **8–9**, 9, 26, **26**, **26–27**, 27, 30, **30**, 58, **58–59**
Sapphires 15, 50, **50**
Schist 25, **25**, 31
Sediment 28
Sedimentary rocks 10, 18, 26, **26–27**, 27, 28
Selenite gypsum 54, **54–55**
Shale 25, 26, 30, **30**
Silver 15, 16, **16**
Slate 19, 25, **25**
South Georgia Island, Atlantic Ocean 24, **24–25**
Specific gravity 41
Staurolite 34, **34**
Steel 17, **19**, 19, 41, **41**
Stonehenge, England 12, **12**
Sulphur 31, 41, 43, **43**

T

Taj Mahal, Agra, India 13, **13**
Tectonic plates 24, **24**, 29, **29**
Tools 12, **12**, 40, **40**
Topaz 39, 50, **50**
Tourmaline 31, **31**, 50, **50**
Travertine **4–5**
Trilobites 52, **52**
Turquoise 15, **15**

U

Ultraviolet (UV) light 40
Uluru, Australia 58, **58–59**

V

Volcanic ash 23, **23**, 29
Volcanoes 12, 22, 29, **29**
    see also Lava; Magma; Obsidian

W

Wegener, Alfred 25
Windows 19, **19**, 38, 43
World
    map of rock resources 16–17

To all the rock hounds of the world who spend their lives digging in the dirt! —ST

Acknowledgment: A special thanks to Barbara Santino for reviewing the text.

Prepared by the Book Division

Nancy Laties Feresten, *Senior Vice President, Editor in Chief, Children's Books*
Jonathan Halling, *Design Director, Books and Children's Publishing*
Jay Sumner, *Director of Photography, Children's Publishing*
Jennifer Emmett, *Editorial Director, Children's Books*
Carl Mehler, *Director of Maps*
R. Gary Colbert, *Production Director*
Jennifer A. Thornton, *Managing Editor*

Staff for This Book

Jennifer Emmett, Priyanka Lamichhane, *Project Editors*
Eva Absher, *Art Director*
Lori Epstein, *Senior Illustrations Editor*
Annette Kiesow, *Illustrations Editor*
Erin Mayes, Chad Tomlinson, *Designers*
Kate Olesin, *Editorial Assistant*
Kathryn Robbins, *Design Production Assistant*
Hillary Moloney, *Illustrations Assistant*
Grace Hill, *Associate Managing Editor*
Lewis R. Bassford, *Production Manager*
Susan Borke, *Legal and Business Affairs*

Manufacturing and Quality Management

Christopher A. Liedel, *Chief Financial Officer*
Phillip L. Schlosser, *Senior Vice President*
Chris Brown, *Technical Director*
Nicole Elliott, *Manager*
Rachel Faulise, *Manager*
Robert L. Barr, *Manager*

Captions

Page 1: Made up of more than 40,000 interlocking columns of basalt, Giant's Causeway in Northern Ireland is the result of a volcanic eruption that occurred more than 50 million years ago.
Pages 2–3: Towering limestone stalagmites form the centrepiece of Furong Cave in the People's Republic of China.
Cover: © Mark Thiessen/ NationalGeographicStock.com
Back Cover: © Sebastian Janicki/ Shutterstock.com

Published by Collins
An imprint of HarperCollins Publishers
Westerhill Road
Bishopbriggs
Glasgow G64 2QT
www.harpercollins.co.uk

In association with National Geographic Partners, LLC

NATIONAL GEOGRAPHIC and the Yellow Border Design are trademarks of the National Geographic Society, used under license.

Second edition 2018
First published 2011

Copyright © 2011 National Geographic Partners, LLC.
All Rights Reserved.
Copyright © 2018 British English edition National Geographic Partners, LLC. All Rights Reserved

ISBN 978-0-00-826783-4

10 9 8 7 6 5 4 3 2 1

All rights reserved. No part of this publication may be reproduced, stored in a retrieval system, or transmitted, in any form or by any means, electronic, mechanical, photocopying, recording or otherwise without the prior permission in writing of the publisher and copyright owners.

The contents of this publication are believed correct at the time of printing. Nevertheless the publisher can accept no responsibility for errors or omissions, changes in the detail given or for any expense or loss thereby caused.

HarperCollins does not warrant that any website mentioned in this title will be provided uninterrupted, that any website will be error free, that defects will be corrected, or that the website or the server that makes it available are free of viruses or bugs. For full terms and conditions please refer to the site terms provided on the website.

A catalogue record for this book is available from the British Library

Printed in Latvia

If you would like to comment on any aspect of this book, please contact us at the above address or online.
natgeokidsbooks.co.uk
collins.reference@harpercollins.co.uk

Paper from responsible sources

Since 1888, the National Geographic Society has funded more than 12,000 research, exploration, and preservation projects around the world. The Society receives funds from National Geographic Partners, LLC, funded in part by your purchase. A portion of the proceeds from this book supports this vital work. To learn more, visit natgeo.com/info.